Pathfinder 25

A CILT series for language teachers

With a song
in my ~~heart~~
scheme of work

Steven Fawkes

As Virgil wrote in the Aeneid Book vii of some learners he knew
(clearly well ahead in curriculum development terms):

'*Ambo florentes aetatibus, Arcades ambo,*
Et cantare pares et respondere parati.'

Both in the flower of their youth, Arcadians both,
and matched and **ready alike to start a song and to respond.**

CiLT

Other titles in the PATHFINDER series:

Being creative (Barry Jones)
Bridging the gap: GCSE to 'A' level (John Thorogood and Lid King)
Communication re-activated: teaching pupils with learning difficulties
    (Bernardette Holmes)
Continuous assessment and recording (John Thorogood)
Creative use of texts (Bernard Kavanagh and Lynne Upton)
Departmental planning and schemes of work (Clive Hurren)
Developing skills for independent reading (Iain Mitchell and Ann Swarbrick)
Differentiation (Anne Convery and Do Coyle)
Drama in the languages classroom (Judith Hamilton and Anne McLeod)
Exploring otherness — an approach to cultural awareness (Barry Jones)
Fair enough? Equal opportunities and modern languages (Vee Harris)
Grammar matters (Susan Halliwell)
Improve your image: the effective use of the OHP
    (Daniel Tierney and Fay Humphreys)
Keeping on target (Bernardette Holmes)
Languages home and away (Alison Taylor)
Listening in a foreign language (Karen Turner)
Making the case for languages (Alan Moys and Richard Townsend)
Nightshift - ideas and strategies for homework
    (David Buckland and Mike Short)
Not bothered? Motivating reluctant learners in Key Stage 4
    (Jenifer Alison)
On target - teaching in the target language (Susan Halliwell and Barry Jones)
Progressing through the Attainment Targets (Ian Lane)
Reading for pleasure in a foreign language (Ann Swarbrick)
Yes - but will they behave? Managing the interactive classroom
    (Susan Halliwell)

First published 1995
Copyright © 1995 Centre for Information on Language Teaching and Research
ISBN 1 874016 45 3

Cover by Logos Design
Printed in Great Britain by Oakdale Printing Co Ltd

Published by the Centre for Information on Language Teaching and Research,
20 Bedfordbury, Covent Garden, London WC2N 4LB.

Contents

			Page
Foreword			1
1. Rationale: making use of the creative contexts			3
A continuum			4
Using songs			6
2. Getting started			7
What sort of songs?			9
Listening for pleasure			11
Listening for purposes			12
Home-made songs			12
Tweaking the familiar			13
When might I use songs?			16
What can I do with songs?			17
Strategies			18
3. My favourite hits			19
1	A song for pronunciation	*Ta Katie . . .*	19
2	A song for physical response	*Ça bouge!*	20
3	A song for joining in	*Salut!*	21
4	A song for sorting	*Hannibal*	21
5	A song for performing	*Gâteaux*	24
6	A song to follow	*Mon, ma, mes*	25
7	A song for amending	*Savez-vous . . ?*	26
8	A song for completing	*Shirley Bassey*	26
9	A song for rebuilding	*La matinée*	28
10	A song for grammar	*Pommes*	30
11	A song for prediction	*Paulette*	32
12	A song for note-taking	*La famille Vabien*	34
13	A song for adding ideas	*Gegenüber der Disko*	36
4. Let's do the show right here . . !			38
Recipe for a home-made song			40
Planning principles			44
Appendix: evaluation schedule			45
Publications and sources			48

Acknowledgements

I am very grateful to the Language Unit at BBC Education for help in producing the audio cassette that accompanies this book.

For their encouragement in the many stages of development of this project I would also like to thank the following colleagues and friends:

Jenifer Alison, Clare Hoogewerf, Stella Marsh, Valerie Miller, Derek Neil, Angela Nichols, Ann Swarbrick, Doreen Smith, Goldenhill Methodist Chapel, all the pupils and colleagues with whom the song activities were developed, and all at CILT.

Foreword

'. . . when a person endeavours to recall (. . .) he is like one who ascends a hill to survey the prospect before him on a day of heavy cloud and shadow, who sees at a distance, now here, now there, some feature of the landscape (. . .) touched and made conspicuous by a transitory sunbeam while all else remains in obscurity.'

W H Hudson

As teachers of languages we are constantly in search of sunbeams which will make the language we are presenting memorable to our class (and provide **us** with a feeling of well-being also).

The purpose of this book is to suggest some practical ways in which we can support learners of foreign languages at any stage in their learning and of whatever sort of ability by framing significant items of language in memorable formats, and by asking them to participate creatively in the work of the classroom. It focuses specifically on the creative context of song, but fits into the broader rationale for involving the imagination and a sense of style as significant aspects of language work.

The combination of familiar bits of language into new arrangements is an important language skill, and the impact of using such language in various situations and novel contexts serves the teacher in making the language involved more memorable.
All of the songs, scenarios and activities described below have been used in French (predominantly) and German classrooms where I have taught, some on many occasions and with different sorts of class, in comprehensive and special schools.

Two caveats at the outset.

- Not everyone responds well to different approaches. I think it is nevertheless worthwhile remaining optimistic, and giving things a try.

- What follows are activities which suit **me** as a teacher, which motivate **me** and which **I** enjoy planning and delivering. I hope colleagues teaching other languages or working on other topics will be able to make use of the underlying principles in their own teaching situations.

The acompanying cassette features some of the songs described in this book, some additional songs and a narrative in which I explain how I have used them. Due to music copyright reasons not all of the songs described in the book are performed, but those that are each have a short gap in front of them to enable listeners to locate them more readily. The cassette is intended to be usable independently of the book, by individual teachers or groups, and the songs themselves may also be useful in the classroom.

To those colleagues who are wary of their own ability to sing in the classroom, my experience is that the effect is not necessarily because it is done well, but because it is done at all.

Steven Fawkes

1. Rationale: making use of the creative contexts

If one of the purposes of language learning is for personal use of the language in a variety of contexts, it follows that, from the outset, learners need **opportunities** to try out their language and gauge its effect; they also need empowerment through **confidence** to try to do something different with the language they know, in order to see it as 'more than a tool for functional/informational purposes' (as Carol Morgan puts it[1]); and they need **awareness** of a range of styles from which to select. The social competences of maintaining the flow of an exchange, entertaining people or just joining in are in need of development (or reinforcement) alongside the purely linguistic skills.

The judicious use of activities based on songs, games and drama may provide some of these opportunities, by demonstrating —
* that a limited amount of language can make a big effect if framed properly;
* and that the little bit of language learnt can be used in more than one way and more than one context.

The principles of a multisensory approach are well established. A variety of learning styles exist; people respond to different sorts of approaches and resources, and teachers plan a wide variety of activities in order to interest the whole range present in classes, maintain motivation, keep attention and reinforce prior learning constantly in different ways. This applies particularly to less able learners whose attention span is often short, and yet who need a great deal of repetition in order to begin to internalise some of the core language they are presented with. The auditory route to learning can be reinforced through the involvement of rhythm, physical activity and tune which are all present in songs.

The strengths of using music to support language acquisition are particularly acknowledged in systems of Accelerated Learning, where the combination of relaxation, baroque airs and aural stimulus can produce significant memory gains. I would have to hesitate personally, however, before exposing my collection of J S Bach to the critical ears of a Year 9 class.

We learn that we can harness more of the brain's power by providing stimulus to its affective and creative hemisphere, by involving the personality, the imagination, music, movement and fantasy and by stimulating the limbic system through emotion and what is pleasing. This power can be invaluable in introducing language into the learner's

---

1. *Language Learning Journal,* 1994

short term memory, where it can then begin to be processed by whatever language device the learner has available.

It seems that the brain's tendency to recall *'features of the landscape'* which are distinctive or unusual could and should be turned to our advantage as teachers. Just as we use visuals to present and recall target language words and expressions, so we can call upon the distinctive strengths of rhythm and music. In particular there is the area of language associated with music in the form of songs, rhymes and indeed jingles, as the hyperbole-manufacturers of the advertising world discovered long ago.

A CONTINUUM

In encouraging the learners' personal involvement with the language we are learning, I hope, as a teacher, to develop three skills, by returning to them regularly:

putting in ideas   **making combinations**   **changing contexts**

In order to be able to participate at the higher levels of creativity and innovation there seems to be some sort of continuum through which learners progress at different rates. To support this progression strategies can be identified by the teacher in the planning of lessons.

Starting with the very basic level of willingness to participate,

this progression may include: . . .   and examples of teaching strategies might be:

⇩   ⇩

- being involved,   provide activities requiring participation.
- responding,   encourage interaction.
- guessing,   accept contributions of all sorts.
- personalising,   allow sink-in and thinking time.
- providing ideas,   demonstrate the brainstorming process.
- asking questions,   be open to queries and suggestions.
- experimenting,   be prepared to join in.
- extrapolating,   show that redrafting can improve on initial ideas.
- innovating,   provide a structure for pupils to work to.

For many of these strategies the use of a song or rhyme can provide an unthreatening context from which to begin. A song played on a cassette can, for example, be the basis for joining in, or for physical response, or for a collective brainstorm before developing words to a new verse.

There are significant planning issues connected with this continuum. Clearly in order to be ready to participate in any sort of activity we all need confidence that we can do so without embarrassment. The classroom atmosphere needs to be positive and imbued with the teacher's own willingness and conviction that what is going on is really interesting.

Many of the messages learners receive about what is expected of them, and what they in turn can expect, come from the general ambience of the classroom and the teacher's attitudes in managing the lesson. For example, as learners experiment with making suggestions or getting a feel for what sounds right in the language, they will make wrong guesses, of course. If such mistakes are not treated sensitively, there is very little motivation for anyone to try again. In order to feel supported, we all need to see the positive aspect of error, accepting wrong guesses not as mistakes, but as steps towards guessing better.

Within any sort of activity requiring people's ideas there is likely to be a requirement for reference skills, to avoid exhausting teacher-demand. At the same time, learners must be trained to use the things they know already (vocabulary, structures, communicative strategies) as the core of their invention, developing some sort of thought process in the target language; otherwise they will simply spend all their time translating their mother tongue ideas word for word with the dictionary, and end up with a hotchpotch of disparate words. This has implications for the amount of structure the teacher provides for learners in early stages of the continuum, the amount of time allowed for individual activities, and for the sort of training offered in coming up with other ideas, making new combinations of words, judging their effectiveness and choosing the best. Strategies for the teacher may include —

- suggesting zany/inappropriate ideas her/himself;
- gapfilling or redrafting activities done with the whole class;
- asking questions, in order to identify alternative ideas, and to gauge personal opinions and reactions;
- experimenting with creative hypothesis 'what if we change X to Y?';
- thinking about improving the quality of work, in terms of style or performance, as well as accuracy.

Again, the context of song has something to offer here, this time in supporting the teacher's confidence as well as that of the learners. With a personally devised stimulus there can, at the outset, be problems or worries about sensitivity. By selecting a pre-recorded song or a familiar tune for the class to work with, the teacher can more readily join in with the class in being critical of the original.

USING SONGS

The nature of a song or verse is that it is made up of sounds and of rhythm. 'Prose' language, as Monsieur Jourdain would call it, is made up of the same elements, but in a less structured format perhaps.

This suggests several ways in which the relationship between spoken and sung language can be supportive:

- We can put the rhythm into a spoken phrase, by clapping for instance.
- We can emphasise where the stress of a phrase lies, by humming its rhythm or by 'conducting' to highlight where the voice rises or falls.

This can be the basis for devising 'rap' phrases (or songs) which have many in-built repetitions, for consolidating purposes.

- We can additionally start from the song, and pick out the rhythm of the language by repeating it.

Finally, and most significantly, songs are intended to be performed and to have an audience, key features of the communicative classroom.

6

2.   Getting started

'Let's start at the very beginning, a very good place to start . . .'

Performance requires an establishment of **confidence** , both on the part of the teacher and of the class.

In order to maintain confidence, whatever the activity, it is important —

- to have a good knowledge of the class and its dynamics;
- to know exactly what you want to get out of the activity;
- to have a good knowledge of the stimulus material;
- to think about how the class will cope;
- to be aware of the mood of the class, the mood of certain key individuals in the class and your own mood.

If the activity involves performance it is also important —

- to plan for everyone to be busy, in one way or another;
- to keep the performance activity short and provide immediate gratification;
- to plan what will happen next, either as the follow-up or as the safety-net activity.

Instead of launching straight into activities involving songs for performance or other high-risk activities, it might be helpful to develop confidence and familiarity with this type of stimulus through a more steady progression. To start with, the class may be listening to the song stimulus, probably more than once, just as they may use a text from their course material:

- listening for key words, in order to match them with a list;
- listening in order to fill gaps in the text;
- listening in order to match the song to a a multi-choice list of possible titles.

Gradually, the distinctive nature of the song-text can be developed:

- listening in order to review a song, maybe giving it a score out of 10 and a comment. (see example below);
- listening in order to identify and then supply words which rhyme at the end of the lines;

- listening in order to identify and repeat the stress of a particular phrase;
- listening to pick out a particular group of words, for pronunciation training;
- listening in order to join in.

Different classes proceed through these stages at very different rates; some are keen to join in from the very first hearing, while others take a long time to be ready. This is one reason why a pre-recorded stimulus can often be much more satisfactory at the outset as it is much easier to rewind and replay, as well as reducing the threat of personal embarrassment by providing a backing track.

Once the class does seem ready to join in with a song, it is important to be realistic about how much they can cope with at a time, and what problems they may have with the lyrics.

The issue of presenting the lyrics themselves will depend upon the reading skills of the class. For many pupils in early stages of reading in a foreign language a request to read the written words, work out how they are pronounced and then reproduce them within the time constraints of a musical phrase can be very intimidating. In such cases it may well be helpful to choose a song with inbuilt repetitions, to focus on one particular phrase for the first rehearsal (or rehearsals), selecting a phrase which is fairly short, fairly frequent in the course of the song and, if possible, which forms a lexical item on its own. This can then be practised, using visual cues if helpful, before the musical reinforcement comes in.

An example from English could be . . .

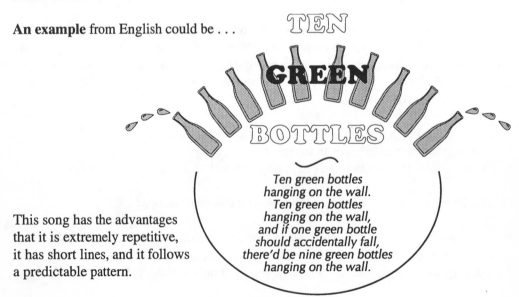

TEN GREEN BOTTLES

This song has the advantages that it is extremely repetitive, it has short lines, and it follows a predictable pattern.

Ten green bottles
hanging on the wall.
Ten green bottles
hanging on the wall,
and if one green bottle
should accidentally fall,
there'd be nine green bottles
hanging on the wall.

For the first hearing the key thing is likely to be the **rhythm** and one or two **sounds**. The second run through may pick out particular **words**, and for the first rehearsal you might select the whole **phrase/line** 'hanging on the wall', as it is repeated several times in the verse, is short, and is fairly complete in itself.

For the second rehearsal, you might take the line *'Ten green bottles'* itself, practise its pronunciation and then use visual clues to ask for ideas of how to say a change of number at the start of the line. During this rehearsal, the class can join in with part of nearly every line in the song.

Finally we are left with the filler-phrases and **the** difficult line, containing the polysyllabic 'accidentally'. This is where the rhythm of the song itself can support spoken skills as we can point out by clapping, tapping or conducting that the stress falls on the first and third syllables of the word, in order to fit the metre of the song. Thus learners have heard in this process that not only are there pronunciation rules governing individual words, but also that there is a certain intonation pattern to be expected when a group of words is put together.

When the whole of the verse is mastered by some members of the class, it can of course, be extended into the verses which naturally follow it. Those who have not got hold of it all by now will have further opportunities to catch up during this extension period. (A German version of this song is included in the Appendix.)

Once the teacher decides that a class is ready to move on to performance activities, the range of activities and of outcomes becomes rapidly much wider.

WHAT SORT OF SONGS?

There is a variety of song material from which to choose according to the particular objectives we have for a specific class, and upon which we can build relevant activities.

- Authentic traditional songs from the target language country;
- Authentic 'commercial' songs;
- Purpose-written songs, linked to published resources;
- Special, home-made songs;
- Songs with actions;
- Recycled songs, building on a model;
- Rap.

Authentic songs from the target language country

What counts as a song?	Where do you get them from?
• Children's songs, traditional songs	Twin schools, friends' families
• Songs from records/cassettes	Scavenging
• Songs from the radio, advertising jingles, theme tunes, raps.	Target language radio and television.

Further sources of authentic songs are to be found closer to home in commercial publications, as well as in the broadcasts of educational radio and television programmes, and of course through networking with colleagues.

What are they like?

Before starting to search for such songs we need to consider what we are hoping to get out of them any way, to establish whether the effort is worthwhile. As they are unlikely to fit particularly well into a language syllabus, it will be necessary to evaluate individual songs in order to judge their usefulness. An evaluation schedule is included in the Appendix.

What are their strengths?

One of the listening skills pupils find most difficult to develop is that of ignoring the insignificant parts of a text they are listening to: they try to work out every single word they hear from the start, and end up frustrated and confused. As a way to put across at an early stage the concept that we do not need to translate or understand everything we hear, an authentic song could be a useful device. We do not, after all, have to worry ourselves needlessly about the rantings of the latest Metal group to enjoy (or otherwise) their performance.

Another strength of authentic resources lies in their great variety of style and of appeal. The question 'Will the class like this song?' should be broadened to take in:

• Will it get a reaction from them?
• Will it illustrate something about the target language culture?
• Is there part of it that has something specific to offer?

Real songs from other countries are usually very rich in cultural detail; everything from traditional songs associated with childhood to the titles in the current chart in a way form part of a nation's civilisation.

As songs are intended either for performance or for listening to, this implies that in the classroom we can use them as both speaking and listening resources. On the one hand they can be used for training people in pronunciation and rhythm by exposing them to the **flow of the song**. Encouraging them to join in and repeat **individual phrases or words** which are appealing can then support this awareness. On the other hand the very nature of musical composition is that it appeals to the emotions (and sometimes the intellect); it is often intended to be heard with pleasure, or to produce a particular response, such as the wish to move or dance.

This seems to have a particular contribution to make to the language learning environment, where, too often,

LISTENING = TESTING.

It could be that the inclusion into a lesson plan of some song material recorded from the radio or from a cassette for very short periods at fairly regular intervals would provide more of a link between —

LISTENING & PLEASURE.

In this case the listening activity would not be linked to the linguistic content of the song or necessarily to the development of oral skills; it would simply be, at the outset, 30 seconds or a minute of listening to something that other people like to listen to. Pupils could gradually begin to offer opinions on what they hear or make comparisons with other songs they know, but in essence this would be a break from the intensive flow of a lesson, possibly a settling activity between two stirring ones.

As such the role of these songs is quite different from that of **purpose-written songs** linked to published resources. Such materials contain songs, rhymes and other performance activities linked to the main language points developed in the resource and are now increasingly available. They are accompanied by activities and strategies for exploitation, and ideally reinforce the overall learning outcomes. (A brief list is included in the section Publications and sources at the back of this book.)

A variety of possible exploitation activities is included in the following chapters.

LISTENING FOR PURPOSES

There are parallels between listening/responding to a song, and listening before producing any piece of spoken language, which are worth consideration.

For some learners the pace of lessons can be very difficult to cope with, and they sometimes do not spend very much time being exposed to one set of language items before they are required to internalise and produce it themselves. It may be that the choral rehearsal of a song can provide a valuable midway point between passive and active participation.

In some ways the musical route from listening only to performance is much more supportive to the individual, as it takes things very much a step at a time. We have a fixed corpus of words we are going to produce; they are always in the same pattern; everyone else is producing the same thing in the same sequence. '*If I can't do it, the rest of the chorus will be there to buoy me up.*' With other forms of oral production the same structure is not available as the dynamics of linguistic interaction in pairwork, groupwork, classwork or individual communication are very much about dealing with the unexpected. '*I don't know exactly what I am going to have to say or what anyone else is going to say back to me.*'

At the point when the relaxed, receptive aspect of listening needs to be converted into the active, participatory aspect of production the problem of the unfamiliar language content of many authentic songs arises once again. Time is, after all, of the essence in a busy scheme of work. It is not only problematical to try to teach a new tune and new words at the same time, it is probably also inefficient to spend any significant amount of time on learning by heart a verse of which the language will not be obviously useful in other situations to be met later on, and one of the key words of our planning as teachers has to be **transferability**.

It is at this point that the home-made song comes into the repertoire, giving, as it does, control of the linguistic and grammatical content to the teacher.

HOME-MADE SONGS

The features of the home-made song are that it builds on what is likely to be familiar to the class anyway, both in terms of the tune 'borrowed' from some other context, and in terms of the vocabulary or other lexical items which they frame.

What counts as a home-made song?

- Tweaked or recycled versions of children's or other songs;
- songs with actions;
- songs based on borrowed tunes: hits (probably of the past!), advertising jingles, theme tunes or traditional songs;
- raps and songs devised by the class, probably to a backing track.

Where do you get them from?

In order to recycle children's songs, it is a matter of taking the original, identifying the key foreign language words we can use to interpret it, and then fitting in other words to fill the gaps!

What are their weaknesses?

They require time for composition, refinement and conversion into classroom-based activities. They also require some imagination and lateral thinking, usually more available when there is more than one brain involved.

What are their strengths?

- The vocabulary and structures presented are purpose-selected;
- their tunes are already familiar;
- recordings are not always necessary. *A cappella* renditions mean that equipment is not needed;
- they are personal. They give the message that creative and entertaining things can be done with the functional or textbook-based language we have learnt together. If I can do it, so can they. (After all, I'm only a teacher.)

TWEAKING THE FAMILIAR

The attraction of editing childhood songs is partly in sending them up and partly in being prepared to participate in something which is recognised as being juvenile.

There is a certain amusement factor in using something familiar since infancy in a different way, as well as a considerable familiarity. The tunes are often wonderful, with lots of possibilities for repetition and personalisation. They are often associated with actions or movements, which can be used to great effect in supporting those (kinaesthetic) learners who need to move about to fix the language they are using.

The *Okey-Cokey,* for example, is a song with obvious links to accompanying actions. This tune seemed to be ideal for recycling into practice of the language for 'finding the way' in German. The following example was for a class in their second year of German, familiar with the direction words, classroom language and vocabulary.

Ist das links?
Ist das rechts?
Links? Rechts?
Rechts? Links?
Ist das links?
In der Stadtmitte,
sprechen Sie lauter bitte!
Links oder rechts?
Oder was?
O bitte, bitte, bitte!
O bitte, bitte, bitte!
O bitte, bitte, bitte!
Links oder rechts?
Oder was?

Steps through the activity (Each key item is accompanied by an action.)

1. Setting the scene
'Ich bin in der Stadtmitte.' (I draw a circle with my finger and point at the middle. The class copies and repeats *'in der Stadtmitte.'*). *'Hier sind viele Autos* (mime), *viele Busse* (mime). *Ich suche die Schule. Hier ist eine alte Person.* (mime) *'Bitte. Wo ist die Schule?'* (mime of dumbshow) *'Ich verstehe nicht. Ist das links?'* (left hand) *'Ist das rechts?'* (right hand) *'Oder was?'* (helpless hand signal) *'Ich verstehe nicht. Sprechen Sie lauter!'* (hand to ear mime) *'Bitte!'* (praying hands).

2. Presentation
Dictate the German phrases to elicit the correct actions from the class.
Perform each of the actions to elicit the verbal response from the class.
Ask individuals to recall the phrases in German to elicit the correct actions from the class.
Hum the tune.
Perform the actions in order. Try to fit the words to the tune.
Sing the song.

3. Performance

If desirable, the written words can be presented in order to improve the performance.

As for **songs based on borrowed tunes**, most of these are very individual, arising from the chance encounter of a concept or linguistic item, and a musical phrase. With practice, they can be searched for more methodically, and a bank of usable tunes can be put together.

It was after a performance of the *Okey-Cokey* above that one of the class suggested we should do another one to a more modern tune, and hit on the theme-tune to *Neighbours*. The assonance of the key-word with the German word 'neben' ('next to' or 'near to') was striking, and it was soon evident that some other prepositions of place, which we had been learning, would fit with this tune, so eminently memorable that my greatest efforts to forget it are to no avail.

Steps through the activity

1. Introduction

Each of the prepositions has a movement associated with it. These have been used previously when we have met the prepositions in context. Here they are presented together orally.

Hört zu! Macht wie ich! Sagt was ich sage!		
WORD	**MEANING**	**ACTION**
auf	on	Hands on head
unter	under	Hands between legs
rechts	right	Point right
links	left	Point left
gegenüber	opposite	Hands point forward and back
vor	in front	Hands in front of chest
hinter	behind	Hands behind back
neben	next to, near to	Hands point to either side
zwischen	in between	Hands to either side of head

2. Linking with the written word

The words are revealed one at a time on the OHP, to encourage the class to read and respond with the appropriate action. They are read aloud for those who do not recognise the written form.

3. Linking with the spoken word

Pupils take turns to say one of the words; the rest of the class (including the teacher) does the required action; any errors in pronunciation are improved at this stage.

4. Performance

The words of the song are placed on the OHP. Hum the tune, or the introduction to the tune, and then sing the words accompanied with the actions.

> *Neben,*
> *gegenüber, auf und neben,*
> *zwischen, hinter, vor und zwischen,*
> *auf und unter, rechts und links.*
>
> *Neben,*
> *gegenüber, auf und neben,*
> *auf, unter,*
> *neben*
> *vor, rechts, vor links.*

5. Spin-off

When the prepositions are needed on future occasions, the appropriate action (with or without the tune) can jog the memory.

WHEN MIGHT I USE SONGS?

- for presentation;
- for practice or consolidation;
- for revision;

- for relaxation;
- for an injection of pace;
- to focus energy.

The question of how often to use songs is very individual to the response of the class and the pressures of a particular scheme of work. Clearly the development of the cultural aspect of the language needs regular and frequent contributions, but these must be balanced against the language objectives and timescale in force. Ideally the content of a worthwhile song will reflect what is in the syllabus anyway, and each topic will have an appropriate musical dimension, used for one of the purposes above.

Songs performed in class are often stirring activities; it is therefore not always right to use them at the end of a lesson, as this can disturb the class's departure. On the other hand, preparation is nearly always involved, so the start of the lesson is not appropriate either. Probably a good moment to move on to a song activity is when the class needs an energising moment, when they may start to be restless with other activities, and when there is still sufficient time to get started on a relevant follow-up activity before the lesson ends.

WHAT CAN I DO WITH SONGS?

In the continuing search for learning outcomes, the teacher finds possibilities in songs —

- to illustrate how rules of pronunciation work, and how they can be stretched sometimes;
- to fix bits of language through the musical auditory route;
- to develop purposeful, accurate copywriting skills;
- to underline selected structures;
- to encourage learning by heart (even if it is subliminal and in spite of themselves for some learners);
- to encourage participation in the whole class, groups or pairs, through actions and through individual creation.

When they enter our classroom pupils are immediately asked to believe themselves in another place, work and talk in different ways, and develop tremendous enthusiasm for whatever the topic of the day is.
Building on the suspension of disbelief inherent in entering a foreign language classroom, as in the theatre, songs offer opportunities to the learners —

- to listen for (what might be a perverse sort of) pleasure;
- to offer opinions;
- to get used to the rhythm of the language;
- to listen and respond in different ways;
- to listen and repeat;
- to perform and earn some applause;

but also at a higher linguistic level

- to listen for a specific purpose;
- to play around with words;
- to predict according to rhymes or syllable count;
- to extend or invent.

STRATEGIES

The strategies listed here are described with practical examples in the next chapter.

Skills	Strategies	Examples
Listening for pleasure	Reviewing	Awarding points to songs
Identifying pronunciation and intonation patterns	Rehearsing	(song 1)
Responding	Listening and doing	Physical response (song 2) Joining in (song 3) Sorting lines in to order (song 4)
	Performing	(song 5)
Linking sounds and writing	Following a text	(song 6)
Picking out detail	Checking a text	Amending verses of a song with a repetitive structure (song 7)
	Completing a text	Adding key words (song 8)
Remembering	Rebuilding a text	(song 9)
Developing a grammatical sense	Repetition of pattern Prediction	(song 10) (song 11)
Making a résumé or digest	Note-taking	Transposing the song into list of key words or phrases (song 12)
Inventing		(song 13)

3. My favourite hits

This is a digest of songs and accompanying activities, used for particular purposes with particular classes. The ages suggested relate the National Curriculum Years and are for guidance only; many of these examples have been successfully used with pupils of different age-groups also. It is my experience that the principles underlying these specific examples can be applied equally to different age-groups and different areas of language.

 A song for pronunciation   **Learners with some linguistic skill**
Year 9/10

Ta Katie . . .

The strategy here is to use the stimulus of the song to focus on particular sounds and their pronunciation, rather than the sense of the words.

This song by Bɔɔy Lapointe is an exhilarating tongue-twister in which the romantic misfortunes of Igor, abandoned by his girlfriend, are narrated by an alarm-clock. The language-level is very high, especially in the verses, but the chorus itself creates a splendid compulsion to try to imitate its pronunciation and rhythm:

Tic tac tic tac
Ta Katie t'a quitté
Tic tac tic tac
Ta Katie t'a quitté

TOC

Tic tac tic tac
T'es cocu, qu'attends-tu?
Cuites-toi, t'es cocu
T'as qu'à, t'as qu'à t'cuiter

TIC

Et quitter ton quartier
Ta Katie t'a quitté
Ta tactique était toc

TAC

2 A song for physical response

Ça bouge

This is a recycled version of the childhood song *One finger, one thumb. . .* The strategy is to build up familiarity with key elements of the song gradually, using physical activity to support the new language.

It is important to remember that we do not need to respond to, or try to reproduce, the whole of a song, or even the whole of a verse straight away. This version of *One finger, one thumb*, for example, would be very difficult for a young class to get into directly. Consequently, learning such a song would need to be spread over several very brief sessions. In practice, at the outset, the focus of the first session could be simply on the refrain *ça bouge* accompanied by a rolling action of the hands; the relevant parts of the body and other actions could then come in gradually over subsequent sessions.

Each line has a corresponding action:

Le doigt et le pouce	pointing with finger and thumb
ça bouge	rolling the hands
un, deux, trois	clapping hands
le bras, la jambe	stick out arm, leg
debout	stand up
assis	sit down

One advantage of a short physically active session such as this can be to refocus the energy of a class when their attention has started to dissipate towards the end of a long lesson. An extension activity can be for the class to suggest further actions which they can fit into the next verses.

ÇA BOUGE

Le doigt et le pouce,
ça bouge,
Le doigt et le pouce,
ça bouge,
Le doigt et le pouce,
ça bouge,
un, deux, trois

Le doigt et le pouce,
le bras, la jambe,
ça bouge,
Le doigt et le pouce,
le bras, la jambe,
ça bouge,
Le doigt et le pouce,
le bras, la jambe,
ça bouge,
un, deux, trois

Le doigt et le pouce,
le bras, la jambe,
debout, assis,
ça bouge,
Le doigt et le pouce,
le bras, la jambe,
debout, assis,
ça bouge,
Le doigt et le pouce,
le bras, la jambe,
debout, assis,
ça bouge,
un, deux, trois

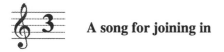 **A song for joining in**

Salut!

The strategy here is to recycle classroom language into a memorable framework, while at the same time suggesting that there are alternative ways of saying similar things. Thus the equivalences between *Comment vas-tu?* and *Comment ça va ?* or *A demain* and *Au revoir* can be pointed out, with similar parallels in the mother tongue. As the amount of language is restricted, it has also proved successful with less able learners.

This song is in the style of the Seven Dwarfs from Disney's 'Snow White', to the tune of 'Hi-ho!'. It lends itself well to being linked to gestures and to being featured at the end of early lessons.

> *Salut! Salut! Salut!*
> *Comment vas-tu?*
> *Moi, ça va bien;*
> *donc, à demain.*
> *Salut! Salut!*

By nature of the original from which this borrowed, the verse then recycles itself until everyone has had enough.

 A song for sorting

Year 8

Hannibal

Songs are intended to be repeated or heard many times. One of the classic strategies for getting to know the parts of a conjugated verb is, of course, drilling; not everyone knows how to drill themselves and certainly not everyone is prepared to spend time on the necessary repetition. By treating the paradigm of a verb as a song, not only is there a context for a great deal of repetition, but also the usefulness of drilling, and some strategies, can be made transparent to the learners at the same time.

This example is for the present tense of the verb *avoir*, and aims to drill the pronunciation of the words as well as their written form. The strategy here is to frame a verb paradigm, which the class needs to know and to note down, in a format which could help them to memorise it, and provide a real reason for writing it down in the first place. The song is the end product of a series of steps intended to reinforce the language in different ways: use of visuals, aural discrimination and matching.

> *J'ai un chat, Hannibal.*
> *Tu as un animal?*
> *Elle a un chien.*
> *Nous avons des poissons.*
> *Vous avez des lions?*
> *Ils ont deux serpents longs.*
> *J'ai un lapin.*

Steps through the activity

1. Introduction
The visuals are presented on OHP or on a poster. The quality of the artwork is unimportant; indeed, the virtue of producing home-made, inaccurate drawings such as mine is that an initial activity can always be to spend some moments brainstorming in order to guess what they are intended to represent! (NB the significance of the speech bubbles and the gender and number of the characters is to relate to the personal pronouns subsequently.)

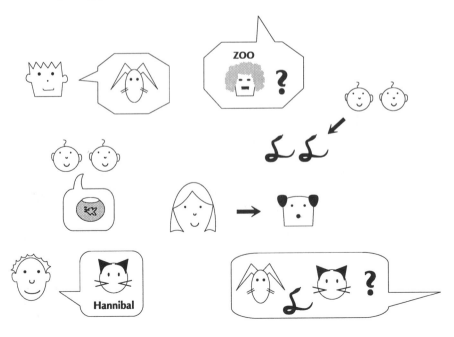

Different question types can be addressed in terms appropriate to the class or differentially to individuals in the class, in order to establish the vocabulary involved.

Plain question   *Qu'est-ce que c'est?*
Gapfill question   *Elle a un ....?*
Complex question *Qu'est-ce qu'ils ont?*

Once the animal vocabulary has been rehearsed or presented, the visuals are shuffled into the order of the lyrics of the song. Each line is labelled with a letter to make the following matching activity straightforward.

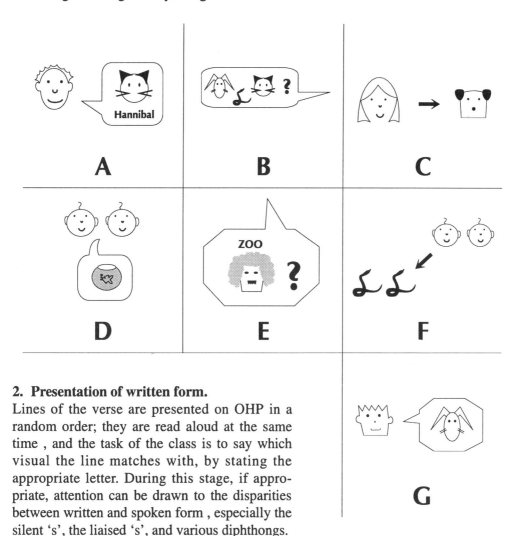

2. Presentation of written form.

Lines of the verse are presented on OHP in a random order; they are read aloud at the same time, and the task of the class is to say which visual the line matches with, by stating the appropriate letter. During this stage, if appropriate, attention can be drawn to the disparities between written and spoken form, especially the silent 's', the liaised 's', and various diphthongs.

- *Elle a un chien.*
- *Nous avons des poissons.*
- *Vous avez des lions?*
- *Tu as un animal?*

- *J'ai un chat, Hannibal.*
- *Ils ont deux serpents longs.*
- *J'ai un lapin.*

3. Performance

Once the lines are arranged, it is appropriate to try to sing the song; it is in the style of the National Anthem.

The various rehearsals which follow provide useful drilling for the class, while the purposeful copying of the song into notebooks can include highlighting of the verb parts, and is consequently both a record of the paradigm, and the stimulus for future performances.

 5   **A song for performing**

Young learners
Year 5/6

Gâteaux

This song was put together in a moderate learning difficulty school for a class of 8-year-olds who had been learning French for only a few weeks. Their curriculum was based on sweets and cakes as key motivating elements of their learning games and activities. The cross-curricular planning of their lessons meant that colours were high on their list of priorities as were numbers which they knew up to 8.

The main point of doing a song was to try to get them all involved in doing something together; secondary objectives were to do with recycling the vocabulary they knew, supporting their pronunciation and having fun.

This is to the tune of *Happy birthday* and was supported by the visuals on OHT. (NB the *e* on the end of *rouge* is enunciated.)

un, deux, trois,	**1 2 3**	🧁 ← bleu
gâteau bleu;		
un, deux, trois,	**1 2 3**	🧁 ← blanc
gâteau blanc;		
un, deux, trois,	**1 2 3**	🧁 ← rouge
gâteau rouge;		
quatre, cinq, six,	**4 5 6**	🍬 🍬
bonbons.		

With a grammatical hat on, I could satisfy myself that at a first level the class had met the concept that adjectives of colour follow their nouns. In fact, they internalised this rule fairly naturally in that particular situation as the significance of the different colourings of cake relate to the school cook's predilection for icing the little buns she sent in at playtime with bright colours; this was language for a REAL purpose!

The children concerned were not in the least bit concerned with the word order, however. They **were** interested in the fact that they could later perform this song in assembly and receive applause for it.

 6   **A song to follow**   **Year 8**

Mon, ma, mes

Some tunes seem to offer themselves as frameworks.
My French classroom poster of possessive words looked like this:

A chance singing of the tune of *Frère Jacques*, seemed to match this quite well, but was not quite satisfactory. The modification of moving the first line to the end seemed to be a much neater arrangement, preserving the rhyme scheme better.

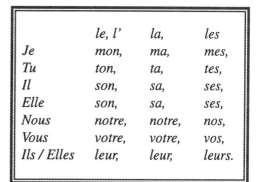

	le, l'	la,	les
Je	mon,	ma,	mes,
Tu	ton,	ta,	tes,
Il	son,	sa,	ses,
Elle	son,	sa,	ses,
Nous	notre,	notre,	nos,
Vous	votre,	votre,	vos,
Ils / Elles	leur,	leur,	leurs.

Mon,	*ma,*	*mes,*
ton,	*ta,*	*tes,*
son,	*sa,*	*ses,*
son,	*sa*	*ses,*
notre,	*notre,*	*nos,*
votre,	*votre,*	*vos,*
leur,	*leur,*	*leurs,*
le,	*la,*	*les.*

7 A song for amending
Year 7/8

Using a traditional song such as *Savez-vous planter les choux?*, a simple listening activity is built around the idea of editing the first verse according to what is heard in the subsequent verses. This can be done using visuals, using cards with the keywords written on them (*nez, pied, main*, etc) or as a gapfilling activity.

(Chorus)	*Savez-vous planter les choux* *à la mode, à la mode?* *Savez-vous planter les choux* *à la mode de chez nous?*
(Verse 1)	*On les plante avec **le nez*** *à la mode, à la mode* *On les plante avec **le nez*** *à la mode de chez nous.*
(Verse 2)	*On les plante avec **le pied*** *à la mode, à la mode* *On les plante avec **le pied*** *à la mode de chez nous.*

In each verse the part of the body changes; after a few examples, the class can begin to make its own suggestions about words they could substitute for those in bold, and then perform these verses to see how they sound.

8 A song for completing
Year 8/9

When pupils are used to handling the written word, they can be asked to manipulate the words of a song as a listening activity. This particular example is a tribute to Shirley Bassey, and can be performed with all the glitter and razzamatazz associated with that singer.

Steps through the activity

Carte de boissons

café au lait
thé
jus de fruit
champagne
whisky avec glaçons
demi-pression
Bordeaux rouge

1. Introduction

This activity is intended to revise some of the vocabulary and functions connected with a visit to the café. It uses the written form of words on a 'carte de boissons', but tries to inject a sense of style into the subject, by framing the language in a glitzy context. The activity begins with study of the 'carte', and the association of the words with flashcards.

2. Participation

The task is that of a collaborative performance. The teacher is the singer; the class is the band, who have to sing the introductory bars in order for the performance to start. The context is that I, the teacher, am the waiter in a café, addressing a female customer, and recommending a range of 'consommations'.

3. Listening and putting in order

The first stage of building up the lyrics for the song is for the class to hear the verse sung through, and to organise the drinks on the 'carte' into the order in which they are heard. This should be checked after the first or second run through, so that the next stage can be done effectively. At this point, the task is to take the functional bits of language presented here and sort them into the order they take in the song. The contribution of the class as musicians pertains.

*vous voulez
peut-être
s'il vous plaît
Mademoiselle
voilà
entrez*

To the tune of 'Hey, big spender!'

*'Mademoiselle, entrez, s'il vous plaît.
Voilà!
Vous voulez..? un jus de fruit?
un champagne?
un Bordeaux rouge?
whisky avec des glaçons?
Un café au lait?
Peut-être du thé?
Un demi-pression?'*

4. Joint performance

If the class is very participative, they may wish to perform the song for themselves now. In any case, extension activities can build on the performance. A second verse can be devised, either in toto, or in order to complete, from a list of potential rhymes supplied, a verse such as the following. In this instance the customer responds; this second role can be taken by a member of the class, if they are confident enough.

Some interesting suggestions for a final line have included the romantic: *'Voulez-vous sortir ce soir?'* and the surreal *'Donnez-moi une pêche et une poire!'*

Further extension activities can include producing a cartoon version of the song, or writing a script with accompanying stage instructions.

 9   **A song for rebuilding**   **Year 8/9**

La matinée

Building on the combination of actions with words and tune, more elaborate linguistic formulations can be framed. The following activity presents those reflexive verbs most commonly needed for talking about the daily routine. As the verses needed to be fairly lengthy to fit in the several syllables of the verbs a popular school hymn suggested itself.

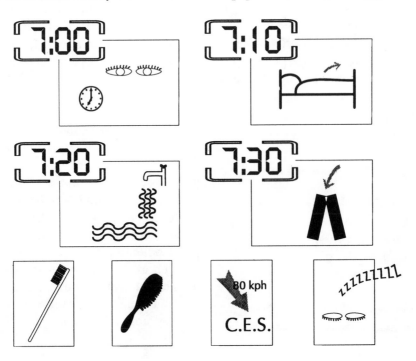

So, in the style of Ancient & Modern, this is to the tune of *Lead me O thou great Redeemer*.

A sept heures je me réveille.
Sept heures dix et je me lève.
Sept heures vingt et je me lave.
Sept heures et demie et je m'habille.

Je me brosse . . .
Je me brosse . . .
Je me dépêche en classe et . . .
Maintenant, je suis fatigué!

Steps through the activity

1. Introduction
Presentation of visuals on OHP and drilling of the related language item: *Je me réveille; Je me lave*. Pupils suggest associated actions. Practice of recognising the language items; pupils perform the actions. Personalisation stage: pupils respond to a visual on the OHP by saying the phrase and adding something to it, if possible. *Je me réveille . . . à sept heures et demie. Je m'habille . . . dans la chambre.*

Presentation: Recapitulation of telling the time, using a digital clockface on OHP. Sample recombination of visuals of time with the other visuals. Pupils practise saying a longer phrase.

Asking for ideas: The visuals are placed one by one on the OHP. Pupils suggest appropriate times to accompany them. This is extended by adding a visual of the Mr. Men character Mr Topsy-Turvy (Monsieur Alenvers). The task now is to provide entirely inappropriate ideas!

2. Preparation of the song
Visuals are placed in the appropriate combination for the words of the song on the OHP; pupils provide the words of the song, line by line, matching it with actions as appropriate.

3. Whole class performance

4. Follow-up
Using the visuals as a prompt, pupils write a draft of the verse, alone or in pairs. This is then checked by a dictation process. Pupils dictate to the teacher what they have written for each line. The teacher transcribes on to the board or OHP, asking for spelling as appropriate and concentrating on significant details, such as reflexive pronouns or unsounded letters. A second draft can then be written up.

A song for grammar   Year 8

> ### *Pommes*

The history of this activity lies in a request to devise a song which would present to a Year 8 class examples of the grammatical rule that *ne . . . pas* is followed by *de* instead of *du, de l', de la',* or *des*. The scheme of work indicated that the vocabulary for this should be 'Fruit', as presented in the coursebook. The consequence was a potential whole new Area of Experience: 'The World of having no fruit'!

Steps through the activity

1. Introduction
'On va préparer une chanson ensemble.' The first stages of this 20 minute part of a lesson were to check on vocabulary of fruit, (with flashcards and realia) and to present examples of the structure in context. To this end we imagined a fairly bizarre situation: I was in the market, my basket was depicted on the OHP, and someone from the class was putting fruit into it. As I was facing away from the screen I could only guess what was in the basket, by asking the class:

'J'ai des fraises?'	*'Non.'*
'Je n'ai pas de fraises. J'ai du raisin?'	*'Non.'*
'Je n'ai pas de raisin.'	

2. Groupwork
We then introduced *Tu as . . .* and moved on to a group activity based on this same information gap exercise. Pupils invented their own basket illustration, and their group took it in turns to identify the appropriate item.

3. Discovering the words
The visual cues below were placed on the OHP, and volunteers suggested what they thought the corresponding lines of the song would be.

4. Recording in writing
A particular concern with this class, as with many others, was their inaccuracy in writing. This showed itself particularly in small, but frequent, mistakes involving *Je* confused with *J'ai*, and omitting the letter *s*. For this reason I asked the class to write down the words **with me,** i.e. watching me form the words on the screen, and keeping pace. I wanted to

point out particular things as they occurred, and to avoid swamping the poorer readers with the whole text in one go. So, as they dictated the lines to me, I wrote them up . . .

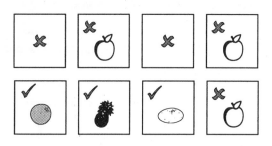

Je n'ai pas . . .
Je n'ai pas de pommes.
Je n'ai pas...
Je n'ai pas de pommes.
J'ai des oranges, des ananas,
des pamplemousses;
Je n'ai pas de pommes.

When completed, we went through the following sequence. I hummed the tune to them once, hummed it again, pointing to the words in time, and then sang the verse through. It is a tribute to the football terraces and has the tune of *We shall not be moved.*

5. Invention by extension

The task of the class in the last few minutes of the lesson was to work in pairs to devise a new verse to this song. During this session the classroom was buzzing with people drilling themselves frantically, as they tried things out. *Je n'ai pas de . . . , Je n'ai pas de . . . , Je n'ai pas de . . .*

Examples

Je n'ai pas
Je n'ai pas de pêche
Je n'ai pas
Je n'ai pas de pêche
J'ai des cerises, des bananes
et du raisin
Je n'ai pas de pêche

Je n'ai pas
Je n'ai pas de prune
Je n'ai pas
Je n'ai pas de prune
J'ai des poires, des bananes
et des melons
Je n'ai pas de prune

6. Further extension

As the song went down well, it returned from time to time throughout the year, and was passed on to other colleagues. Much later on, I met one teacher who told me her class had had considerable fun doing the same activity with 'clothes' vocabulary. Their favourite chorus had been: *Je n'ai pas de slip*!

Another example of extension

The extension activity does not need, of course to relate exactly to the song-context from which it springs. With another class who learnt this song, pressure of time suggested it would be appropriate to consolidate the recognition of the pattern *ne . . . pas + de* by setting a short written homework activity. For this, a new Mr Men character was invented and illustrated in a cartoon. *Voici Monsieur Napas.*

The homework task was to create another cartoon about Monsieur Napas, using the same structure, for display on the classroom noticeboard.

Monsieur Napas regarde Neighbours . . .

. . . mais il n'a pas de télévision!

 11   **A song for prediction**   **Year 10/11**

This activity exploits the features of rhyme and syllable count within a verse. It is really for older learners, to rehearse rules connected with the perfect tense and to involve people in coming up with ideas and making suggestions.

Steps through the activity

1. Introduction
The verse is on OHT. ' *Voici un vers. Il y a des mots qui riment.* '
An example of rhyming words can be given to ensure the concept is clear.

2. Presentation
The verse is revealed, and read aloud, line by line on the OHP; the words marked with stars are covered up with slips of paper, and only revealed when they are correctly identified. '*J'ai mangé chez Paulette; j'ai pris ma* ✶✶✶✶✶✶✶✶✶'. When the hidden words are reached in the text, a syllable count can help to suggest an appropriate word. Suggestions can be stored on the board for a follow-up activity, or just for comparison with the original. Some of the gaps to be filled are nouns; the articles preceding these gaps are useful cues, reminding learners of basic elements of grammar to do with gender. Other gaps are verbs, or parts of verbs, and the process of filling the gaps can focus on their formation, including the agreement of the past participle.

A table!

(Version on OHT)	(Complete version)
J'ai mangé chez Paulette;	*J'ai mangé chez Paulette;*
j'ai pris ma ✶✶✶✶✶✶✶✶	*j'ai pris ma serviette,*
choisi sauce tomate	*choisi sauce tomate*
avec mon ✶✶✶✶✶✶✶✶.	*avec mon omelette.*
J'ai mis la moutarde	*J'ai mis la moutarde*
et la mayonnaise;	*et la mayonnaise;*
j'ai bu du sirop -	*j'ai bu du sirop -*
du sirop à la ✶✶✶✶✶✶.	*du sirop à la fraise.*
J'ai pris ma serviette;	*J'ai pris ma serviette;*
j'ai dit 'Bonne ✶✶✶✶!'	*j'ai dit 'Bonne fête!'*
Sur mon assiette	*Sur mon assiette*
j'ai vu une ✶✶✶✶!	*j'ai vu une bête!*
Je l'ai dit à Paulette	*Je l'ai dit à Paulette*
et elle a crié.	*et elle a crié.*
J'ai été surpris;	*J'ai été surpris;*
mon assiette est ✶✶✶✶✶✶!	*mon assiette est tombée!*
Cette bête (à trois ✶✶✶✶)	*Cette bête (à trois têtes)*
a ✶✶✶✶✶ *mes frites.*	*a mangé mes frites.*
Je me suis levé,	*Je me suis levé,*
mon sirop est ✶✶✶✶✶,	*mon sirop est tombé,*
et je suis parti tout de suite!	*et je suis parti tout de suite!*

Follow-up

This verse is sung to the tune of Julie Andrews' *My favourite things*. Nearly all of the final *es* are voiced. The words can alternatively be learnt or read as if they were simply a poem or tongue-twister. The text can also be transposed from 1st to 3rd person, to see if the same rhythm can be retained. The alternative suggestions stored on the board can be used to make up new verses to the song, either in class or at home.

La famille Vabien

This is sung to the tune of *Auld Lang Syne*. The words are as follows:

> *Anne est la mère;*
> *c'est Pierre, le père;*
> *des deux enfants Vabien,*
> *La fille est Claire;*
> *le fils, Robert,*
> *et Bruno, c'est le chien.*

However, before reaching the stage of hearing the song, I would like the class to help me assemble the lyrics using visual prompts, so that we can then use the same prompts to sing it subsequently, without having the interference of the written form of the words. Furthermore, at the end of the activity session I want them to use the visuals and a variety of reference items to record the words of the song accurately. Firstly, I want to reinforce the differences between *le* and *la* words in order to remind them of that most difficult concept, that everything has a gender in French.

For this I use a simple 'sorting sheet' on the OHP, like this:

m.		f.

Steps through the activity

1. Introduction

i. *'On va faire une chanson sur une famille. C'est la famille Vabien. Voici Pierre, Bruno, Anne, Claire, Robert.'*
Show the names on the OHP, one at a time.

ii. Put the pictures, one at a time, onto the OHP. Pupils guess which name goes with the picture, in order to practise pronouncing the names.

iii. Grammatical section. *'Pierre est le père de la famille. C'est Monsieur Vabien. Anne est la mère. C'est Madame Vabien.'*
Use the 'sorting sheet' to place Pierre's picture in the 'Masculine' box; then Anne's into the 'Feminine' box. Do the same for the children of the family, teasing out a response from the class as to whether your choice of box is correct. The class should now have visual support for grouping the *le* words together and the *la* words together. The question of where to put the dog now arises! Hopefully the cue word *le chien* will be sufficient to guide the class to the right conclusion about its gender.

(This same activity can subsequently be extended and reused for any vocabulary set just to keep reminding people when they are thinking of a word for *the* they do have a choice to make.) The sorting sheet is kept available for the end of the activity session, when the class takes its own notes.

2. Building up the lyrics

'Comment s'appelle la mère? Et le père? Et la famille? Il y a combien d'enfants? Comment s'appelle la fille? Et le fils?' The class has now heard the key language several times and a quiz should allow the words to be put together in the right order. When the correct answer is forthcoming, the teacher confirms it with the appropriate line of the song, i.e. *'Comment s'appelle la mère?'* *'Anne'* *'Oui, Anne est la mère.'* In this way the verse is put together. It works quite nicely if the last line is not presented until the first performance to the tune, at which time there is a certain satisfaction when the lyrics actually fit!

3. Performing the song.

The tune is introduced simply by humming it. Personally, I like to perform the song first by myself with the class joining in if and when they can, but that stage can possibly be omitted. Depending on the class, their recall of the song may be stimulated solely by the visuals, if it is rehearsed enough; otherwise, the written form may need to be presented beforehand.

Pronunciation skills: there is always a risk of interference when pupils read with their non-French-speaking eyes and speak accordingly, but sufficient unscripted preparation beforehand can be coupled with specific attention to difficult letter-combinations and words (*c'est*, *enfants*) in order to raise awareness of the conventions of French pronunciation.

4. Follow-up
The issue of following up a song activity is dependent on the class and their response to the song. In order to make the most out of our training with *le* and *la* the class should now make their own notes on the song, using key words, e.g. '*Anne — la mère, Pierre — le père*' etc.

However, alternative plans are sometimes required with different sorts of classes.

- Some groups might be asked to copywrite the whole verse at this stage.
- Another group might like to make a class recording.
- For another group further questioning provides a brainstorming activity about the characters in the song. '*Quel âge . . ?*' '*Qu'est-ce qu'il/elle aime faire?*', etc, which leads into a creative writing activity.
- For yet another group the task is for pairs to come up with either a new verse to the song, or a verse about a different family.

 13   **A song for adding ideas**   **Year 8**

Gegenüber der Disko

In order to begin to test what they can do with the language they know learners need to begin from a supportive structure, with enough framework that they can see what is expected of them. There are few things more intimidating than a blank page and instructions to fill it!

The following activity involved pupils in putting in new ideas into a preordained structure. It is quite a short activity that fitted into a sequence of other approaches within a lesson to do with German prepositions and their cases in the context of places in town. The majority of the lesson was taken up with:

Whole class stage:
- OHP presentation of visuals;
- presentation of words, and matching with visuals;
- manipulation of visuals, using prepositions (*rechts von dem Rathaus*);
- spotting the links between the preposition and the sound of the article following it (*neben **der** Post*);
- trying to predict the link;
- looking at the written form of the words.

Pair work stage
- jigsaw activity with the written forms (*neben der +?*);
- information gap activity based on a town plan.

Individual work:
- reading activity based on the same language;
- writing activity based on the same language.

In order to change the context, and to draw the class back together, a tribute to Judy Garland was introduced based on a blackboard picture. It is to the tune of *Somewhere over the rainbow*.

> *Gegenüber der Disko,*
> *vor dem Park,*
> *neben einer Toilette*
> *hier steht Mark.*

In order to move into an idea-suggesting stage, this verse requires a very specific brainstorming session; after all, there are only a limited number of people's names that actually rhyme with the names of places in town!

Examples

> *Vor der Jugendherberge*
> *hier ist die Post.*
> *Neben einem Sportszentrum*
> *ist Frau Kost.*

> *Gegenüber der Kirche*
> *vor dem Platz*
> *neben einer Toilette*
> *ist Herr Fatz*

> *Zwischen der Jugendherberge*
> *und dem Park,*
> *hier ist die Fußgängerzone,*
> *neben Mark.*

37

4.   Let's do the show right here . . !

Learners inventing

There can be many purposes to which the stimulus of a song or verse can be put in the classroom, and the same stimulus can be used equally well with younger pupils or the less able as with older pupils or the more able if the activity associated with the song is challenging at an appropriate (cognitive) level.

Although invention of pieces of language in a song format can be seen at the end of the line of progression, this line can be shorter or longer, depending on the support provided. Learners can be led into inventing or creating their own verses and songs at various levels, from '*arrange these lines into a sequence you like*' through '*substitute new words (or lexical items) for those highlighted*' towards '*produce a verse of your own*' and even at this level the difficulty of the task can be varied to suit the situation:

- invent to fill a gap (either at the level of individual words, or of a whole line);
- invent to extend;
- invent to imitate the format of the stimulus;
- invent to fit a certain length of the line (for a collaborative effort, for instance);
- invent to fit the metre pattern;
- invent to fit a rhyme scheme;
- invent to fit a tune;
- invent a verse on a topic;
- invent in a particular style (e.g. a radio jingle).

The nature of the work produced can also be focused by the objective of the activity:

- inventing in order to publish will produce the need for an accurate piece of writing;
- inventing in order to perform will produce the need for fluency and clear articulation;
- inventing in order to record will produce the need for high quality voices and probably accompaniment.

Au café

A class of Year 8 pupils was learning about going to the obligatory café in France. In order to get them to try out new combinations of words and rehearse pronunciation, the tune of *Old MacDonald* proved very useful in providing a new context for their practice language, and for putting in new ideas.

Steps through the activity

1. Introduction

This was set up as an anecdote using as a prop an extremely stale croissant. *'J'entre dans le café. Je dis bonjour. Le garçon arrive.'*

'Monsieur? Vous désirez?' *'Je voudrais une tasse de café. s'il vous plaît.'*

'Avec un croissant?' At this point the displeasing aspect of the croissant is made extremely apparent.

'Non, merci. Une tasse de café.'

'Avec un croissant?' There follows a great deal of repetition and some farce. Symbols are placed on the OHP to stimulate recall of the words.

2. Performance (NB The *e* of *une* and *tasse* are enunciated).

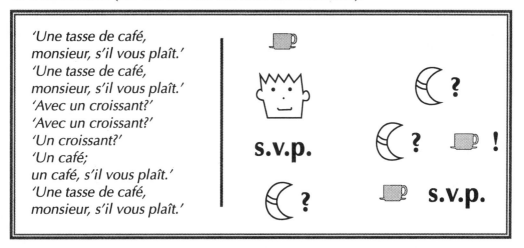

'Une tasse de café, monsieur, s'il vous plaît.'
'Une tasse de café, monsieur, s'il vous plaît.'
'Avec un croissant?'
'Avec un croissant?'
'Un croissant?'
'Un café; un café, s'il vous plaît.'
'Une tasse de café, monsieur, s'il vous plaît.'

3. Follow-up

i.   Applause is required. The supportive atmosphere of the classroom needs to operate in all directions.

ii. The symbols are used for the class to perform the song, firstly in chorus, then with different groups taking the roles of the customer and the waiter.

iii. A whole-class brainstorm session makes some initial suggestions for a second verse. Different food and drink items can be tried, along with other ideas; observations on how a suggestion sounds are made at a very basic level, and alternatives can be tried out. By humming the tune and counting on their fingers, pupils can begin to think about syllable-count.

iv. In order to liberate those pupils who can cope with a less rigid structure, a hypothesis is introduced to those groups: *Dans le café, il n'y a pas de garçon; il y a une fille . . .* They suggest what changes will need to take place accordingly.

v. A few minutes only are spent with a partner coming up with a new verse. This activity needs to be brief to avoid the problems of ideas becoming too elaborate or of dictionary interference.

Examples

A pair of girls opted for the waitress in their café, necessitating a complete redraft, as *Mademoiselle* takes up more space than *Monsieur*. Their refrain was:

> *'Mademoiselle, s'il vous plaît.'*
> *'Une tasse de thé.'*

A pair of boys presented me with their paper upon which was written the single word 'bière'. Taking my puzzled silence for expectation they went straight into a rendition:

> *'Une biè-è-è-è-re,*
> *Monsieur, s'il vous plaît.'*

Perhaps this counts as 'Differentiation by outcome'?

RECIPE FOR A HOME-MADE SONG

1. First catch your tune. Open a file on memorable tunes that may come in some time. Familiar tunes (if possible lousy ones; they're less threatening and more memorable) include:

i.	Childhood tunes:	very flexible as they tend to be repetitive.
ii.	Songs from the shows:	the big film musicals offer lots of inspiration.
iii.	Hits of the '60s, etc.:	rhythmic and upbeat.
iv.	Carols and hymns:	depending on the background of your school.
v.	Tunes from the TV:	adverts and theme tunes are designed to be memorable.

i

Ten green bottles
Old MacDonald
Auld Lang Syne
Twinkle, twinkle, little star
Three Blind Mice
Charlie is my darling
One man went to mow
She'll be coming 'round the mountain
Greensleeves

Examples:

ii

White Christmas
Climb every mountain
Supercalifragilicexpialidocious
Singing in the rain
(or almost anything by
Julie Andrews)

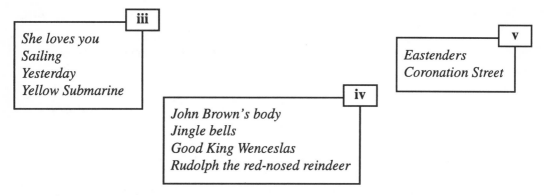

iii

She loves you
Sailing
Yesterday
Yellow Submarine

iv

John Brown's body
Jingle bells
Good King Wenceslas
Rudolph the red-nosed reindeer

v

Eastenders
Coronation Street

2. Secondly, choose between the inspirational route (2a) or the task-solving route (2b).

2a.   Look/listen for any assonance between a word in the original and a key word in the target language. Look also for conceptual links. Sometimes a pattern in the first line of the song makes a lateral connection with a phrase in the target language, and starts the words flowing into their framework.

2b.   Decide what parcel of language you want to frame in a song. Look/listen for a tune with the right sort of syllable count per line. Think of possible alternative wordings you can use, in case the original phrase proves problematical. When fitting words into the framework, be flexible. Without compromising rules of intonation, pronunciation and syntax it is often possible to find a different order of words or change the selection of words slightly to reach a more satisfactory conclusion. Be prepared to abandon a cherished phrase if it just won't fit. Look for possibilities of rhyming words.

Example

The task was to find a way to present the articles *au, à l', à la, aux* with examples in a memorable framework.

i.   The hunt for a song with similar sounds in it, led from *à l'* to *The Alleluia Chorus*.

ii.   A list of possible examples was compiled: *à l'église, à l'école, au garage, aux magasins, au syndicat d'initiative, à la mairie.*

iii.   Looking for rhyming words suggested that *garage* would benefit from *plage* and *village* as rhymes.

iv.   Fitting the words to the tune indicated that many of the musical phrases are quite short (4 beats) but also highlighted the need for one very long phrase linking the verses.

v.   Trial and error led to the decision about which lines to make rhyme. After manipulating the possibilities for a while, there seemed to be a state when the verse felt all right. It can later be amended in the light of experience of course.

The first verse ended up so: *A la plage;*
                                au garage;
                                à l'école;
                                au village;
                                à la gare.   with the final *e* enunciated once again.

There were more examples to be incorporated, however, and the class could cope with a broader vocabulary base than this. A variation produced a new verse with some more difficult combinations of sounds:

                                A la plage;
                                au garage;
                                à l'agence . . .
                                de voyages;
                                à l'hôpital.

This was where the long phrase was needed (10 beats). Which places might fit here? *A l'Office de tourisme* was too short, as was *au syndicat d'initiative.* Fortunately, the police station came to the rescue with its syllable count and its intonation intact:

                                Au commissariat de police;
                                à l'église;
                                à l'église;
                                à l'église;
                                à l'église.

The National Library has a different intonation pattern, meaning that the *la* needs to be slightedly swallowed to keep the flow going:

                                A la Bibliothèque Nationale
                                à la piscine municipale;
                                à la piscine municipale.

It's then back to the same short format lines as above:

                    A la plage;   *A la plage;*
                    au garage;   *au garage;*

à l'agence . . .	*à l'école;*
de voyages;	*au village;*
à l'hôpital.	*à la gare.*

There is a sense of intellectual satisfaction when everything seems to fit in its place. However the problem in practical terms turned out to be that not very many of my pupils were well up on their Haendel. (See 'Beware' below.)

Bear in mind

- The less new language you include, the more digestible the song will be, the more impact it will have on first hearing, and the more rapidly it can reach performance.

- The first bit of a tune is very flexible; for example, you can always hum yourself an introduction if your words don't start until halfway through the line.

- In French it is a convention that the *e* which is usually mute on the end of a word can be enunciated at the end of a verse, if it helps.

- If the musical line is too long you can make one syllable last for several notes, but this sounds odd unless it is significant syllable. For example, it sounds all right to stretch the main syllable of a word like *trente*, but not the *e* at the end.

- You will want to exploit the impact the song makes straight away; what sort of follow-up will be appropriate?

- Do you want to link lyrics with actions or visual cues, or make the link with the written word clear?

- How will the song activity fit with your classroom practice?

Beware

 If the length of the musical line is too short there is a tendency to swallow syllables, make uncomfortable contractions and change the natural flow of the language. This is to be avoided, as there is obviously no point in learning it wrong. Intonation and pronunciation rules should be respected.

 It's worth doing some research or brainstorming before you commit yourself to a particular tune. You may be the only person in the hemisphere who knows all the words to your chosen anthem!

Appropriateness
Pace
Accessibility
Practicability
Mixed Skills
Expectations
Enjoyment

- There are times when the introduction of a song activity is particularly appropriate. Any sort of excess or imbalance is to be avoided!
- The audience for the type of activity outlined above tends to thrive on a mixture of familiarity and variety, and performs best in activities which are **short** enough to be accomplished within their attention span. The issue of **pace** within a lesson also comes into play here.
- Any activity must be unthreatening (for teacher and pupils) as well as **clear and accessible.** If there is any risk of people getting lost, by accident or design, this has to be remedied.
- This can be clarified by identifying **clear objectives** for the activity. This helps teachers know what they want (listening for pleasure or for review, joining in, writing down, adapting or inventing) and helps them stay within the limits of what is achievable in the time available.
- The principles of **mixed skills** apply here as elsewhere in activity design; there should be opportunity not just for hearing or singing a song, but also for following it up, building on it, or extracting something from it.
- A word about the teacher's own performance: the reaction of individual classes to different sorts of approaches is fairly unpredictable, however, it is probably best to **expect** some laughter if you burst into song unexpectedly. This is partly from surprise, partly from embarrassment, but is really part of the game, and should be built on as a positive stimulus for further enjoyment. Teachers uncomfortable with singing themselves frequently could make use of a backing tape (with or without the words) to support the activity. Similarly, there are things to **expect** about the performance of the class: reading the words and saying or singing them is hard, as two processes are involved at once. The use of short lines, visual clues and much drilling can be anticipated.
- Finally, the major principle behind all the preceding is that of **enjoyment,** looking for angles on what needs to be done anyway, in order to put it across in a way in which learners and teachers can share a sense of pleasure in one aspect of the manifold uses to which people put language.

Appendix

Evaluation schedule

In the interests of making effective use of classroom time, the following schedule may be useful in focusing attention on the merits or problems of using a particular song.
(NB As I am the person who is going to have to present the song to the class and carry them along with my own enthusiasm, I put my own opinion at the top of this list! Clearly if the answer to questions 2 or 3 is 'No' the song will go into the decent oblivion that awaits all exhausted *Eurovision* entries. If the song does make it on to the lesson plan, I will need to ascertain the response of the class afterwards, of course.)

SONG TITLE: _____

1. What is this song like?
    ----

2. Do I like it?
    ----

3. Will class X like it?
    ----

4. Will another class like it?
    ----

5. When does it seem to fit into the scheme of work?
    ----

6. Will I use all of it?
    ----

7. When will I use it in the lesson plan?
    ----

8. What will I use it for?
    ----

9. How will I use it?
    ----

10. What will the learner/teacher gain from this?

Example

Quand trois poules vont aux champs,
La première va devant;
La deuxième suit la première;
La troisième vient la dernière.
Quand trois poules vont aux champs,
La première va devant.

SONG TITLE: *Quand trois poules vont aux champs*

1.	What is this song like?	*Jolly*
2.	Do I like it?	*Yes*
3.	Will class 7A like it?	*Yes*
4.	Will another class like it?	*?*
5.	When does it seem to fit into the scheme of work?	*Unit 8*
6.	Will I use all of it?	*Yes*
7.	When will I use it in the lesson plan?	*End of lesson*
8.	What will I use it for?	*Confirmation of ordinal numbers, place words*
9.	How will I use it?	*Visuals of hens, numbers to manipulate on OHP, play tape, join in*
10.	What will the learner/teacher gain from this?	*Bit of fun*

Example

Vive le vent, vive le vent,
vive le vent d'hiver
qui s'en va en courant
dans les grands sapins verts.
Vive le vent, vive le vent,
vive le vent d'hiver.
Boule de neige,
grands sapins blancs
et bonne année, grand-père.

SONG TITLE: *Vive le vent* (tune of 'Jingle Bells')

1.	What is this song like?	*A bit difficult*
2.	Do I like it?	*Yes*
3.	Will class 8B like it?	*Maybe*
4.	Will another class like it?	*Y7, other Y8*
5.	When does it seem to fit into the scheme of work?	*Christmas*
6.	Will I use all of it?	*Yes*
7.	When will I use it in the lesson plan?	*Start of lesson, end of term*
8.	What will I use it for?	*Mainly for pleasure, maybe some pronunciation work with more able groups*
9.	How will I use it?	*'-ent, -in, -ant' sounds*
10.	What will the learner/teacher gain from this?	*Cultural reference*

Publications and sources

'Ta Katie t'a quitté' words and music by Boby Lapointe, 1964. © Editions musicales INTERSONG TUTTI, 74, bd de la gare, 75013 Paris

Song cassettes published by **MGP/Stanley Thornes**:

> *Chanterelles*
> *Chantez OK!*
> *Singspiel*

BBC Radio and Television series regularly include authentic and purpose-written songs. Examples:

> *Jeunes Francophones (TV 1994)*
> *Le Club (Radio and TV 1995)*
> *Radio Relax (Radio 1995)*
> *Radio Aktiv (Radio 1995)*
> *Radio Ondas (Radio 1995)*
> *Deutschlandspiegel (Radio 1995)*

In particular the beginners' television series *Hallo aus Berlin (TV 1996)* features ten songs, the lyrics of which were written by the present author to match the core linguistic content of the programmes.

Collins E, *Le français, c'est facile!: French songs for special educational needs* (John Murray, 1995): supports Brown S and S Dean, *Le français, c'est facile!: strategies and resources for special needs* (John Murray, 1995).

Elston T, P McLagan and A Swarbrick, *Génial* (Oxford University Press, 1995): uses a regular Karaoke feature on its cassettes to support.

Jenkins B and B Jones, *Spirale 2* (Hodder and Stoughton, 1992): set of three cassettes accompanies the book; cassette C is *Spirale musicale*.